paris and nicole's guide to
the simple life

PENGUIN

PENGUIN BOOKS

Published by the Penguin Group
Penguin Books Ltd, 80 Strand, London WC2R 0RL, England
Penguin Group (USA) Inc., 375 Hudson Street, New York, New York 10014, USA
Penguin Group (Canada), 10 Alcorn Avenue, Toronto, Ontario, Canada M4V 3B2
(a division of Pearson Penguin Canada Inc.)
Penguin Ireland, 25 St Stephen's Green, Dublin 2, Ireland (a division of Penguin Books Ltd)
Penguin Group (Australia), 250 Camberwell Road,
Camberwell, Victoria 3124, Australia (a division of Pearson Australia Group Pty Ltd)
Penguin Books India Pvt Ltd, 11 Community Centre, Panchsheel Park, New Delhi – 110 017, India
Penguin Group (NZ), cnr Airborne and Rosedale Roads, Albany, Auckland 1310, New Zealand
(a division of Pearson New Zealand Ltd)
Penguin Books (South Africa) (Pty) Ltd, 24 Sturdee Avenue, Rosebank 2196, South Africa
Penguin Books Ltd, Registered Offices: 80 Strand, London WC2R 0RL, England

www.penguin.com

First published 2004
1

Copyright © Twentieth Century Fox Film Corporation, 2004

Text by Amanda Li

Set in Bad Dog
Made and printed in Italy by Printer Trento SRL

British Library Cataloguing in Publication Data
A CIP catalogue record for this book is available from the British Library

ISBN 0–141–38187–6

Well, they did it! Paris and Nicole achieved their goal of living the simple life (twice over) and, boy, did they learn a lot along the way. Like where to find hot guys in the middle of nowhere, how to get real intimate with a cow's behind and why you should never go nude once you're over thirty — the wrinkled-suit effect is just so not flattering.

Want to find out all the other things the girls learned? Well, take a look at Paris and Nicole's most memorable moments, getting flirty on the farm and rockin' on the road. These girls are simply the best!

Even in the middle of nowhere, you can still pull a fellow party animal.

When heading off to the country, don't forget to pack your chauffeur — just in case you need him.

It may not be the **Hilton**,
but sleeping next to a
well has its advantages.
It's not great for **beauty sleep**,
but it's handy if you want some
fresh spring water in the middle
of the night.

Playing around with younger guys is so much fun.

When you suffer from CAD (Charging Account Disease), almost any kind of shop is a temptation — even a local food mart.

You'll only attract dogs in a rusty old pickup truck. The best pickups are large, pink and shiny.

Hitting the bottle isn't nearly so much fun on a farm as it is in Beverly Hills.

Hay! Ditch the dungarees.
Reunions are a blast —
and you get to wear heels.

Feeling part of the community and mixing with the locals can be so stimulating. They're hot!

When stripped of cash and credit cards, you need to live off your wits and flirt shamelessly with useful guys, regardless of age or class.

When you have a particular skill or talent, it's only fair to use it as much as possible. Especially when your parents are paying.

It's good to try
something completely new.
Cleaning up your act can be
great — and you get a
maid-to-measure skirt
thrown in.

Always aim for perfection – even with the **humble sausage.** There is such a thing as the perfect **size, width and length.**

Detail is everything.
Never, repeat, never,
miss an opportunity to
check your hair
and make-up.

Rise to a challenge. When you've only ever painted your nails, it's hard to get on a roll. But if you run out of wall stuff, you can always visit some place called Walmart.

Don't be afraid
to take risks —
but never with
your own hair.

A little **power** can
go to a **girl's** head.
You're like
so busted, baby!

Never underestimate your worth. Since this cow had a celebrity makeover, it's been charging for personal appearances.

It's all over — and it feels so good to be back home. Paris and Nicole are reunited with their families and their credit cards. Where would they be without them?

Never forget, girls:

KEEP IT SIMPLE!